RACING CARS

RACING CARS

by Robert B. Jackson

illustrated with photographs

NEW YORK / HENRY Z. WALCK, INC.

629.22   Jackson, Robert B.
   J   Racing cars.   Walck, 1970
                63p.   illus.

                Sequel to: Sports cars.
                Description of each of the important
             types of cars raced in the U.S. and
             how competition is organized.

                1. Automobile racing   I. Title

ISBN:0-8098-2072-2

LIBRARY OF CONGRESS CATALOG CARD NUMBER: 73-124112

PRINTED IN THE UNITED STATES OF AMERICA

Acknowledgments

The author wishes to thank the organizations that provided photographs for use in this book:

Ford Motor Company, page 62; Goodyear Tire & Rubber Company, page 36; Daytona International Speedway, pages 27, 29 and 32; National Hot Rod Association Photo Service, photographs by Leslie Lovett, pages 15, 38 and 40; Oswego (N.Y.) Speedway, page 34; Porsche-Audi Division of Volkswagen of America, Inc., page 45; USAC News Photos by D. Lynn Justis, pages 13, 20, 22 and 24; Valvoline Oil Company, page 41; Pud's Atlantic Station, Waterbury, Conn., p. 30.

Other photographs are by the author.

Contents

1   *The Exciting World of Automobile Racing,* 9

2   *U.S. Automobile Racing Organizations,* 11

3   *Track Racing Cars,* 19
       INDIANAPOLIS CARS, 19
       SPRINT CARS, 21
       MIDGET CARS, 23
       GRAND NATIONAL STOCK CARS, 25
       LATE MODEL SPORTSMAN STOCK CARS, 28
       MODIFIED STOCK CARS, 30
       GRAND AMERICAN STOCK CARS, 31
       SUPERMODIFIED STOCK CARS, 33

4   *Straight Line Racing Cars,* 35
       LAND SPEED RECORD CARS, 35
       DRAGSTERS, 37
       SUPER STOCK CARS, 39
       FUNNY CARS, 41

5   *Road Racing Cars,* 43
        GROUPS FIVE AND SIX CARS, 43
        PRODUCTION SPORTS CARS, 46
        TRANS-AMERICAN SEDANS, 48
        CANADIAN-AMERICAN (GROUP SEVEN) CARS, 50
        CONTINENTAL CARS, 53
        FORMULA VEE CARS, 57
        FORMULA FORD CARS, 58
        GRAND PRIX CARS, 59

6   *Off-Road Racing Cars,* 61

1 / The Exciting World of Automobile Racing

Racing cars are fascinating and exciting automobiles. Their bright colors, sleek lines and trim purposeful design set them apart, even when they are at rest.

In motion they are all the more spectacular. They scream down the straights and dart through the turns, with engines roaring, tires whining and dust swirling behind them. And they often race wheel-to-wheel or nose-to-tail, with each driver pushing his car to the limit in an effort to lead the speeding pack.

Such flashing action and stirring competition has made automobile racing increasingly popular in this country. Thousands of new fans are being attracted by the thrilling sport; a number of additional tracks and courses have recently been built; and the U.S. automobile

/ 9

racing calendar is now crowded with many lively events.

But some of these recent enthusiasts—not to mention a few of the older ones as well—are occasionally confused by the wide variety of cars that are raced in the United States. There are stock cars and Indianapolis cars, dragsters and midgets, sports car and formula cars, cars that have their engines in front and those having engines in rear, even cars that run on special fuels as compared to cars that race on gasoline.

If the situation were not already bewildering enough, several classes of automobile sometimes race in the same event. On the other hand, similar cars occasionally compete in different styles of racing. And finally, rival racing organizations have been known to give different names to the same cars.

Little wonder, then, that many automobile racing fans are unsure of themselves from time to time. They are not always certain just who is racing against whom, for what award, and in what class of car. This book is intended to show the many kinds of U.S. racing car, tell how they differ from one another, and explain the basic organization of their rousing and dramatic sport.

2 / U. S. Automobile Racing Organizations

In the past, U.S. automobile racing was much different from European motor sport. Americans raced round and round on oval tracks; while Europeans preferred competition over open roads or on closed courses that imitated open roads. Since World War II, road racing has become popular in the United States as well, however.

A third style of motor racing, straight line competition, has also become more common in this country in recent years. Originally straight line racing meant trying for a land speed record. In attempting to set a land speed record, a single car races in a straight line over a standard distance against the clock. Such attempts have been made in the U.S. from time to time ever since the automobile was invented.

But now straight line racing is much better known here in the form of drag racing. When drag racing, two cars accelerate from a stop over a straight quarter of a mile.

Separate controlling organizations have been set up within each of the three styles of U.S. automobile racing. These organizations determine technical specifications for the cars allowed to compete in their events and license the qualified drivers. They also schedule racing dates for the tracks, courses and drag strips affiliated with them. And, of course, they conduct the races and give the prizes as well.

Track racing nearly always involves one of two kinds of car. Track cars are either open-cockpit, single-seater, all-out racing cars; or they are stock cars, which look pretty much like street automobiles. Each of these two types of oval competition has its major organization. The United States Auto Club is primarily for the pure racing cars; and the National Association for Stock Car Auto Racing controls the stockers.

USAC is only for professional drivers and has its headquarters in Indianapolis, Indiana. As might be expected from its location, USAC sanctions the best known U.S. automobile race, the annual Indianapolis 500. Not as well known is the fact that the Indy 500 is only one of a series of twenty or so USAC races for Indianapolis-type cars. This series is held each year throughout the country to determine a USAC national champion.

USAC has additional divisions and championships for sprint cars and midgets. They are open-cockpit racers that are not as large or as fast as Indy cars. There is also a USAC division for late-model stock cars. This division

Track racing is still the most popular form of U.S. motor sport. These are USAC midgets running on a flat quarter-mile oval inside the Astrodome, Houston, Texas.

has never been very strong, however, USAC's chief concern being the traditional open-wheeled racing car.

The major power in stock car racing is the National Association for Stock Car Auto Racing, based in Daytona Beach, Florida. NASCAR has four divisions for professionals and a Hobby section for amateur drivers. In the past the fastest NASCAR stockers, the Grand National division, have raced mostly on the big superspeedways of the Southeast. Now they are gradually expanding their competition into the rest of the country as well. The Grand American (small sedan) division still runs nearly all of its races in the Southeast. The other two NASCAR pro divisions, Sportsman and Modified, are represented on numerous small tracks on many parts of the United States.

Besides USAC and NASCAR there are several other track racing groups in the U.S. None of them is as large; and most of them are regional in nature. Many small "outlaw" tracks also exist which operate independently of any authorizing organization. These smaller groups and outlaw tracks have often been the training ground for young and inexperienced oval drivers.

The two rival groups organizing drag racing are NHRA, the National Hot Rod Association; and AHRA,

Drag racing is a straight-line, quarter-mile acceleration test for two cars at a time. This pair of dragsters is competing in the NHRA Winternationals at Pomona, California.

the American Hot Rod Association. NHRA, the larger of the two, is located in Los Angeles, California; while AHRA has its headquarters in Kansas City, Missouri.

Drag racing is easy to understand after the cars are off the line. One car is pitted against the other in a simple test of acceleration. But the system of classifying these cars before they race is confusing, to say the least. Almost

Unlike evenly shaped ovals or straight-line drag strips, road courses are full of twists, turns and even hills. Pictured are SCCA Trans-Am sedans on the Lime Rock course in Connecticut.

one hundred classes have been set up to give a wide variety of automobiles a chance to compete fairly. Within each of these classes, winners go against winners until all but the fastest have been eliminated. The survivors then drag each other in seven categories called "eliminators."

A small group of full-time pros tour the big drag meets; and the number of part-time professionals is considerably larger. By and large, however, most drag racers are amateurs.

Most road racing in the United States is supervised by the Sports Car Club of America, which has its offices in Westport, Conn. Because SCCA was strictly an amateur racing organization for many years, the larger part of its racing schedule is still made up of amateur events. Successful graduates of SCCA weekend drivers' schools are then licensed for local racing. If they run responsibly at that level, they can earn licenses entitling them to step up to National Championship competition.

About sixty such SCCA National races are held each year in various parts of the country. At the end of the season the top finishers in each class of cars from seven geographical regions are invited to compete in the American Road Race of Champions. Winners of the ARRC are then regarded as the U.S. amateur road racing champions for that year.

SCCA has also undertaken a strong professional racing program recently. The Trans-American series features road racing for small sedans; and the Continental series is road racing for single-seater, open-wheeled cars. Most important of the three SCCA professional championships is the Canadian-American Challenge Cup, which is contested by big international two-seater sports racing cars.

Besides its amateur program and three professional series, SCCA also sponsors four U.S. road races that are part of international championships. Three are endurance events for two-seater racing cars which count toward the International Manufacturers' Championship; and the fourth is the important United States Grand Prix. The United States Grand Prix is part of a world-wide series for Grand Prix cars, usually thought of as the most advanced form of motor sport.

Rules for international races are made by the Federation Internationale de l'Automobile in Paris. The national automobile clubs of seventy countries belong to the FIA, the United States being represented by a committee. This committee is called ACCUS, the Automobile Competition Committee for the United States. Not surprisingly, the four members of ACCUS are delegates from USAC, NASCAR, NHRA and SCCA.

So much for the background—and alphabet—of big-time automobile racing in the United States. Now let's step out from behind the pit rail and have a look at the cars themselves.

3 / Track Racing Cars

Loud, colorful and extremely fast, USAC's Indy cars are also called Championship automobiles. They run a long season, racing in such places as Trenton, New Jersey; Phoenix, Arizona; and Riverside, California, as well as at Indianapolis on Memorial Day. Championship cars compete on both dirt and paved tracks, and road courses as well. Lately the number of dirt events has been decreasing, and road races have been getting more common.

Indy cars cannot be longer than sixteen feet and must weigh at least 1,350 pounds. Their current design is based on that of European Grand Prix cars to a large degree; and they are low, rear-engined, and appear to be all tires. (Seventeen inches is the current width for the rears.)

Engines based on mass-produced types are allowed in Indy cars as well as engines built just for racing. Super-charging, or pumping additional air and fuel into the engine for greater power, is also permitted. USAC has established a variety of maximum engine-sizes to make performance as equal as possible. The largest is for un-supercharged "stock-blocks," while supercharged racing engines are required to be smallest.

At present the most successful track engines are the turbocharged racing Fords and Offenhausers. (A turbo-

charger is a simplified supercharger operated by the engine's exhaust gases.) Such engines are held to 161 cubic inches in size.

(Engine size, also called displacement, is a measurement of the total cylinder space through which the pistons travel. The higher the number, the bigger the engine. And, other things being equal, the bigger the engine, the greater its power.)

Championship racing is the pride of USAC; and no other organization races the Big Cars, as they are sometimes called. Brutally fast and demanding to drive, they can exceed two hundred miles an hour on the longer straights. In 1970 Al Unser averaged 155.749 mph in this Colt-Ford (photo) to win the Indianapolis 500.

Sprint Cars

Indy cars are low and dart-shaped with their engines in the rear, but sprint cars are high and bulky. Their engines are still up front; and the deeply scooped cockpits are located back near their stubby tails. The drivers sit bolt upright and are clearly visible to the fans while racing. In contrast, not much more than the tops of the drivers' helmets can be seen in Championship cars.

Sprint cars were first built in the 1920's as smaller

versions of Indianapolis automobiles. Most Indy cars have changed radically in design since then; but sprint cars have remained pretty much the same. This is because they are still perfectly suited to the rough half-mile dirt ovals on which they generally run. (While not nearly as many Championship races are held on dirt as formerly, Championship dirt cars are still built to this older pattern as well.)

USAC's engine sizes for sprint cars are roughly equal to those for Indy cars; but the smaller organizations running sprint cars have no limitations on engine size at all. Although Offenhauser racing-type engines were the rule in USAC sprint racing for many years, the most popular engine at present is the stock-block Chevrolet. Like their Indy big brothers, sprint cars burn alcohol-based fuels.

Although Indy cars must have a wheelbase of at least eight feet, the distance between the axles of a USAC sprint car cannot be over seven feet. This gives the "three-quarter" cars greater maneuverability on shorter tracks. They storm around half-mile ovals at such places as New Bremen, Ohio, or the Reading, Pennsylvania, Fairgrounds, turning hundred-mile-an-hour laps on the faster tracks during qualifying. (In comparison, the fastest qualifying speed for the 1970 Indianapolis 500 was over 170 mph.) Spectacular on the dirt, sprint cars power-slide wildly through the turns, spouting great clouds of dirt behind them and hanging their tails so far out as to be almost sideways on the track.

Midget Cars

Midgets are even smaller variations of the front-engined, open-cockpit racing car. Except for their reduced size, they look very much like sprint cars and they powerslide through turns in the same exciting way.

USAC midgets have wheelbases only five feet six inches to six feet four inches in length, and wheels a mere twelve or thirteen inches in diameter. Many have Offenhauser engines which are scaled-down versions of the Indianapolis originals. Such midget racing engines cannot be over 114 cubic inches in size, 76 if supercharged. A few USAC midgets have stock-block engines from Ford Falcons or Chevy II's, and they are allowed a maximum size of 155 cubic inches.

Midgets are most at home on quarter-mile tracks, where they usually qualify at something like seventy miles an hour. The biggest event of their seventy-five-race USAC season takes place during March in Houston, Texas, where a special quarter-mile dirt track is built just for the night inside the famous Astrodome. (See photograph, page 13.)

Besides USAC, several regional clubs also organize midget cars; and other groups race even smaller cars. The three-quarter or TQ midgets generally run indoors on tenth-of-a-mile tracks; and the quarter-midget class is for youngsters. These tiny cars have a four-foot wheelbase, about a three-horsepower engine, and a top speed of perhaps twenty-five miles an hour.

GRAND NATIONAL STOCK CARS

NASCAR's flashy Grand National stock cars are the big league of stock car racing. Each year they run a dozen or so long races on big banked superspeedways as well as many short races on smaller tracks, mostly in the Southeast.

The first event of the Grand National season is a road race (unusual for NASCAR) at Riverside, California, in January. Then in February comes the biggest race of the year, the Daytona (Florida) 500. Other highlights of the Grand National schedule are a six-hundred-mile race at Charlotte, North Carolina, in the spring and the Southern 500 at Darlington, South Carolina, on Labor Day.

Up to two years old, Grand National cars run on pump gas and still look like the mass-produced sedans they once were—but only on the outside. Inside, it is a different story. The original engine, body, brakes and suspension have all been modified for much greater strength and speed. A minimum weight of 3900 pounds has been specified by NASCAR; and beginning in 1971 the engine can be no larger than 366 cubic inches. The minimum wheelbase allowed is nine feet, eleven inches. At Talladega, Alabama, the fastest of NASCAR's super-speedways, booming Grand National cars have qualified at nearly two hundred miles an hour.

Grand National races are usually won by the big factory-supported teams rather than the smaller independents. In recent years the chief rivalry has been Fords and Mercuries against Plymouths and Dodges. At the end of the season a national champion driver is determined by a point system based on the finishing positions of each race. The car in the photograph is a Ford Talladega.

LATE MODEL SPORTSMAN STOCK CARS

NASCAR Late Model Sportsman stock cars are sedans that were originally built between 1955 and the two-year-old cut-off date for Grand National cars. Late Model Sportsmen are allowed greater mechanical changes than cars in the Grand National division—for example, the engine does not have to be the same year as the rest of the car.

Like Grand National cars, Late Model Sportsmen must run on gasoline. Only one carburetor (a device that feeds gasoline into an engine) is permitted. The wheelbase is required to be a minimum of nine feet, seven inches; and Late Model Sportsmen are required to weigh at least nine pounds for each cubic inch of engine size.

Biggest race of the busy LMS schedule is the Daytona Sportsman 300 (photograph), a preliminary event to the famous Grand National Daytona 500. Both races are run on the big two-and-a-half-mile banked tri-oval in Daytona Beach, Florida. The fastest qualifying speed for the 1970 Sportsman 300 was 181 miles an hour in a 1966 Ford. (The fastest 1970 Grand National qualifier did 194 mph in a 1969 Mercury.)

Modified Stock Cars

NASCAR's Modified division is for steel-topped automobiles going back as far as 1935, but not as recent as Grand National cars. Modifieds are allowed many mechanical changes, more than even Late Model Sportsmen.

There are few limitations on Modified-engine size; and engines can be swapped around within a manufacturer's line. Multiple carburetion, or even the more advanced system of direct fuel injection, is also allowed. Superchargers can be used, and anything goes for fuel. Among the few restrictions are a minimum weight of 2,900 pounds and a minimum wheelbase of nine feet, one inch.

The thousands of outlaw stock cars being raced all over the United States most nearly resemble entries in the NASCAR Modified division. For years the favorite bodies for both NASCAR and outlaw Modified competition were Ford, Mercury and Chevrolet two-door coupes from just before World War Two. These lightweight bodies are now becoming hard to find, however, and NASCAR has recently run races for only Late Model Modifieds.

One of the biggest races for the Modifieds is held each October on a one-mile track in Langhorne, Pennsylvania. In 1969 the fastest qualifier there ran a record lap of more than 116 mph in a 1937 Ford.

The photograph shows a Modified that runs in unsanctioned open competitions in New England.

GRAND AMERICAN STOCK CARS

The relatively new Grand American cars were first raced by NASCAR in 1968. They are compact high-performance sedans such as Barracudas, Firebirds, Javelins and Mustangs. Sometimes called "Baby Grands" in the stock-car press, like Grand National cars they can be up to two years old. A maximum engine-size of 305 cubic inches is specified (as compared to the Grand Nationals'

366), and the wheelbase can be no longer than nine feet, four inches (Grand National minimum: nine feet, eleven inches). Otherwise the restrictions are much like those for Grand National competition.

Grand American races were first promoted as preliminaries to Grand National races. They are now popular enough to attract their own enthusiastic fans to many of NASCAR's smaller tracks. To keep the competition equal, NASCAR does not permit Grand National drivers to race Grand American cars. The most successful Grand American entries to date have been Camaros (photo); and a winning car will usually average from seventy to eighty miles an hour over a hundred-mile race.

Supermodified Stock Cars

Supermodified stock cars are not authorized by any national organization, but well-attended supermodified races are conducted on a local basis in many parts of the country. Because their competition is not organized, there are no overall specifications for supermods. Mostly, however, they are of two types.

The first type look like the wildest of Modified stock cars, changed even further. Just about anything goes mechanically, the engine not having to come from the same manufacturer as the frame or body, for example. Extreme body changes are also allowed, fender removal and drastic lowering being only the beginning. But however much they have been changed, the basic parts of these supermods were originally stock.

The second type of supermods are essentially old sprint cars. A big, production-based engine (usually a Chevy V-8) is dropped into the front; and an inverted wing is often rigged on the roll-cage over the cockpit. The roll-cage protects the driver in case the car turns over; and the wing increases the traction of the rear wheels by causing air pressure to push them downward. Some fans think these supermodifieds have an unfair advantage because they are based on all-out racing auto-mobiles instead of stock cars.

The fastest supermodifieds can turn lap speeds of over one hundred miles an hour. Their biggest race is held in the fall at Oswego, New York, where the photograph of this wingless "caged-sprint" was taken.

4 / Straight Line Racing Cars

Land Speed Record Cars

The first American to set a world land speed record was Henry Ford. He did 91.37 mph for the flying mile on the ice of Lake St. Clair, Michigan, in January of 1904. He built the record-setting car himself.

From then until the mid-1930's, such attempts were made on the sands of Daytona Beach, Florida. By then, however, the record already exceeded 275 mph, too fast for the location. Further trials have since been made on the smoother and more spacious Bonneville Salt Flats of Utah.

This is Craig Breedlove's "Spirit of America," in which he set a long-standing record of 600.601 mph on November 15, 1965, at Bonneville. The "Spirit of America" had a turbojet aircraft engine, was over thirty-four feet long, and weighed four tons.

DRAGSTERS

The "Christmas tree" light pole between the two lanes blinks amber for the fifth time. Before the green bulbs can flash—but not soon enough to "red-light" and stop the run—the pair of dragsters explode from the "hole."

Their wide rear tires lay down black rubber and the frail front wheels bounce high in the air as the dragsters' big engines shriek to almost ear-shattering levels. Trailing thick white clouds of bitter smoke and spitting blue flame, the two AA/Fuel dragsters blast down the strip.

AA/Fuel dragsters are the fastest accelerating automobiles in the world and are capable of speeds over 225 mph by the end of the quarter mile. (Actually drag fans prefer a statistic that summarizes an entire run rather than just final speed. They talk about "E.T.," which means elapsed time, start to finish. Fast AA/F cars are now "in the sixes," running a quarter mile in less than seven seconds.)

The engine of a AA/F dragster is usually a big Ford or Chrysler. Because it has been totally rebuilt with special parts and been supercharged, it can produce a staggering 1500 horsepower during its brief run.

AA/F dragsters burn nitromethane mixed with several other easily vaporized liquids like acetone and benzine. Such a mixture would be too expensive, too explosive and much too wearing for family automobiles; but it makes AA/F cars about a second quicker than the similar AA/D dragsters which burn gasoline.

There is little more to a dragster than its massive engine and a long spidery frame to hold the wheels. The goggled and helmeted driver wears a flameproof suit,

gloves and mask, and hunches in a tiny cockpit behind the rear wheels. Because of the long frame and the drivers' position, dragsters are sometimes called "rails" and "slingshots."

Stopping such fast vehicles in a short distance can be a real problem. Because ordinary brakes would not be up to the task, dragsters are brought to a halt at the end of their run by popping big parachutes from their tails.

SUPER STOCK CARS

Another very popular dragging category is called Super Stock. Unlike specially built dragsters, Super Stock cars are basically high-performance street automobiles such as Barracudas, Camaros and Mustangs. NHRA has twenty classes for Super Stock cars, and also divides them into professional and amateur groups.

As in other NHRA categories, the various classes reflect the weight of a car as compared to the size of its engine. NHRA also separates cars having automatic transmissions from those with manual gearboxes. The best of the fastest class of Super Stocks have E.T.'s well under ten seconds.

Fans like Super Stocks because they look much like the cars they drive themselves. Automobile manufacturers are therefore highly aware of the advertising value of good drag performances and support their own Super Stock teams. The car in the photograph is a Camaro.

Funny Cars

Funny cars received their name before they were officially recognized. They are street automobiles that have been modified so drastically they formerly did not fit into any class and could not compete. They proved so interesting, however, that a special class was eventually created for them.

Although they look like street models, funny cars perform more like dragsters. Besides extensive mechanical changes, they have special fiberglass bodies which are lightweight copies of the usual metal ones. The driver often sits in what was originally the back seat (photo);

and funny cars burn fuel instead of gasoline. As a result, the quickest funny cars run in the low sevens, over 200 mph.

Organized drag racing began in California, and much of the sport remains centered there. But the number of major drag races held each season throughout the country is still increasing as the popularity of dragging continues to grow. NHRA's "Big Four" meets have customarily been the Winternationals, the Springnationals, the Nationals and the World Finals.

5 / Road Racing Cars

GROUPS FIVE AND SIX CARS

The Federation Internationale de l'Automobile (FIA) establishes the rules for automobile racing on the international level. These regulations apply primarily to road racing, because track and drag racing are relatively rare outside the United States.

Among other events, the FIA organizes a series of long-distance endurance races called the International Manufacturers' Championship. This series includes races in Great Britain, Italy, Belgium, Canada, Austria and Germany, the most famous being the Twenty-Four Hours of Le Mans, held in France each June.

Three races in the United States also count toward the International Manufacturers' Championship. They are the twenty-four-hour race at Daytona in January; the Sebring (Florida) Twelve Hours in March; and a six-hour race at Watkins Glen, New York, in July.

As the title suggests, the championship for this series is awarded to the manufacturer of the car scoring the most points rather than to a driver. The series is contested by two of the nine groups of cars that the FIA has recognized.

Group Five includes the two-seater racing cars the FIA calls "Sports Cars." There is a language difficulty here, because these automobiles are *not* the nimble little street cars we notice darting along the highway. Instead, they are vastly expensive, all-out racing cars of very limited production. They are usually raced only by factory-supported teams and never seen in parking lots. German Porsche 917's (photo) and Italian Ferrari 512's are examples of Group Five cars.

Group Six is for prototypes, which are two-seater racing cars of which only one of a kind need have been built. The French Matra 650, the Ferrari 312 and the Porsche 908 are Group Six cars. No current U.S. car is racing in either Group Five or Six, although outdated Ford GT-40's still occasionally run in Group Five as "Sports Cars."

The cars in both groups must have two seats, enclosed wheels and regular doors, starters and windshield wipers, and working brake- and headlights. In addition, Group Five "Sports Cars" must carry a spare tire and have luggage space of a required size. These restrictions date from the time that the FIA raced street-type sports cars in its long-distance events.

The maximum engine size for Group Five "Sports Cars" is 305 cubic inches; and for Group Six Prototypes

it is 183 cubic inches. Current design favors engines located just in front of the rear wheels, and both groups run on pump gasoline. Although reliability is more important than small differences of speed in endurance racing, Group Five cars reach two hundred miles an hour on the straights.

Group Four cars, those the FIA calls "Grand Touring" automobiles, also compete in the Manufacturers' series. But because they *are* what we know as sports cars (Corvettes, Porsche 911's, an occasional MGB, etc.) they are much slower than Groups Five and Six and are not serious contenders for overall honors.

At present the chief rivalry for the International Manufacturers' Championship is between Ferrari and Porsche. Porsche was the winner in 1969 and 1970, the car in the picture being the 1970 Daytona-winning Group Five Porsche 917. This blue and orange wedge-shaped 917 averaged almost 115 mph for twenty-four punishing hours of racing.

PRODUCTION SPORTS CARS

The largest number of U.S. automobile road races are authorized by the Sports Car Club of America for its amateur racing program. The greatest number of cars competing in these races are production sports cars. Production sports cars are mass-produced, street-type sports cars, such as Alfa-Romeos, Corvettes and Triumphs, that have been specially adapted to racing. In the early days of SCCA road racing such cars were driven to the course, raced, and then driven home. Nowadays, however, they are so highly tuned they must be trailered to and from the race.

SCCA has divided its production sports cars into eight classes, ranging from A to H, based on potential speed. Class A (primarily Corvettes and Cobras) is fastest; and Class H (mostly Sprites) is slowest. In 1969 on the tight, twisting mile-and-a-half course at Lime Rock, Connecticut, the record Class A lap was 88.5 mph, set by a Cobra (photo). A Sprite held the Class H record at 80.8 mph.

SCCA races for production sports cars are usually short, running ten laps or so for regional events and half an hour in length for the more important Nationals. More than one class of cars often compete at the same time; and SCCA spectators need sharp eyes to keep track of the races within a race. Since road courses are generally in the country, and it takes nearly a day for a typical SCCA racing schedule, most fans combine their race-watching with a camping trip or picnic.

Trans-American Sedans

SCCA divides sedans into four classes by engine size for amateur road racing; and sedan racing is always part of the usual SCCA Regional or National race weekend. More importantly, SCCA also sponsors a professional series of sedan races that has become so popular with racing enthusiasts it is now heavily supported by U.S. automobile manufacturers. Officially named the Trans-American Championship, but usually called just the Trans-Am, it consists of a dozen or so races on road courses all over the United States.

Trans-Am cars are quite similar to NASCAR's Grand American class, being compact sedans such as Chevrolet

Camaros, Dodge Challengers, Ford Mustangs, Pontiac Firebirds and American Motors Javelins. Like NASCAR, the maximum engine size is 305 cubic inches. Unlike NASCAR, however, Trans-Am cars run on the road and are allowed only one carburetor.

At each Trans-Am event, SCCA also holds a preliminary race for small sedans with engines less than 122 cubic inches in size. Italian Alfa-Romeo GTA's and German BMW 2002's usually contest the lead in this race; but the rivalry is even more bitter in the larger class. The

already rough battle between Mustangs and Camaros has recently been expanded by the entry of factory-backed Javelin, Barracuda and Challenger teams.

The fans especially like Trans-Am racing because the familiar-looking cars are very fast for their size and weight. The fastest lap during qualifying for the 1970 Lime Rock Trans-Am was 93.5 mph (a Javelin) as compared to the Class A sports car record of 88.5 mph. And since Trans-Am races generally last for about three hours, there are also whirlwind pit stops for gasoline to excite the spectators and sometimes determine the outcome of the event. In the photograph (page 49) is a Plymouth Barracuda.

CANADIAN-AMERICAN (GROUP SEVEN) CARS

SCCA sports racing cars are two-seater, closed-wheel automobiles that have been built solely for road racing. Usually much faster than production sports cars, they are generally constructed in limited numbers by small manufacturers. SCCA divides them into four classes by engine size for amateur competition.

Technically, FIA Groups Five and Six cars would be eligible for this category; but they race almost exclusively on the international level for the Manufacturers' Championship. However, SCCA's Class A for sports racing cars pretty much corresponds to the FIA's Group Seven: sports racing cars of no minimum weight with engines of unlimited size. And SCCA started sponsoring a series of professional international races for these big Class A/Group Seven cars in 1966. Since then the Canadian-American Challenge Cup (Can-Am, for short) has grown rapidly to become the richest and most publicized group of road races on the U.S. schedule.

With total awards of more than a million dollars for an annual series of ten or eleven races in the United States and Canada, the Can-Am attracts the fastest cars and drivers from all over the world. The cars are lightweight, European-type chassis powered by huge modified American engines in the rear. This combination of superior handling, favorable power-to-weight ratio, and vast power make Can-Am cars among the quickest of road racing automobiles. On long straights they are capable of well over 200 mph.

The thundering engines and blazing speed of Can-Am competition are now thrilling thousands of spectators each year from Edmonton, Albèrta, to Bridgehampton, New York. Nearly all Can-Am cars currently use

Chevrolet engines, while the most successful chassis to date has been the McLaren (photo). The late Bruce McLaren, a New Zealander, originated the car in England and drove one of his own orange Team McLaren McLarens himself. Either Bruce or teammate Denny Hulme won all eleven Can-Am races in 1969.

Single-seater, open-cockpit racing automobiles are called "formula cars" in Europe. This is because the FIA establishes a set of rules, or formula, for each of three classes of such cars: Formula One, Formula Two and Formula Three.

The term has been carried over into SCCA usage; and SCCA has also set up three classes for formula cars: A, B and C. Formula C cars have engines smaller than 67.1 cubic inches in size. The engines of Formula B cars are between 67.1 and 97.6 cubic inches; and Formula A allows engines from 97.6 up to 305 cubic inches.

All three classes compete in SCCA's amateur road racing program; and there is also a professional series for SCCA formula cars called the Continental Championship. About a dozen events are held each season for the big Formula A cars, with combined preliminary races for Formulas B and C. SCCA names driving champions in both divisions at the end of the series.

The majority of the chassis for Formula A Continental cars are built in England, McLarens, Lolas and Lotus being popular choices. Almost all Continental Formula A cars have a stock-block Chevrolet V-8 in the rear, carefully rebuilt and modified for much greater speed. Such engines are quite similar to those used in Trans-Am Camaros.

Distinguishing features of Continental cars are the very wide rear tires and the wings mounted on stilts over the rear wheels. Like the wings on supermodified stock cars, these airfoils use the pressure of the air to help "get the power to the road."

Although the Continental series was only started in 1967, it has already become a highly important part of the U.S. road racing program. Prize money and lap speeds have both increased rapidly each year; and spirited competition among several teams for the championships has attracted many new fans.

Like most U.S. road races, a Continental begins with a rolling start. Arranged by qualifying times, the competitors slowly tour the course behind a pace car. When they reach the start-finish line a second time and get the green flag, the drivers stand on the gas and rocket into the first turn, wheel to wheel. Continental A cars are now sizzlingly fast, the Lime Rock Formula A lap record having been set in 1969 by a Surtees T55 (photo) at 105.7 mph.

FORMULA VEE CARS

SCCA also sponsors a formula that is at the opposite end of the scale from the big Continental cars. Known as Formula Vee, it is for small, open-cockpit racers built from Volkswagen parts.

The class is held strictly to stock VW parts by SCCA; and most of the drivers build their own cars from kits. This makes Formula Vees relatively inexpensive; and the class is a favorite of beginning SCCA drivers.

The most popular SCCA class in number of entries, the little "bugs" are also exciting for spectators to watch. Because they are so similar in construction, the Vees usually stay bunched together throughout an entire race with several drivers contesting the lead at every chance. Vees are not all that slow, either; the fastest Vee at Lime Rock being only about two seconds a lap slower than the fastest Cobra.

Formula Vee is based on the 72.7-cubic-inch engine, brakes and suspension of 1966 VW's. These parts are now becoming hard to find; and in 1970 SCCA created a Formula Super Vee derived from current 97.6 cubic-inch Volkswagens. Greater freedom of construction is also allowed within this new class, making Super Vees considerably faster than Vees.

Formula Ford Cars

Formula Vee, which originated in the United States, is now raced in Europe. In reverse order, Formula Ford began in England and is now recognized by the SCCA. Based on 97.6-cubic-inch English Ford Cortina engines (the same size as Super Vees) and modified FIA Formula Two chassis, Formula Fords are also a closely competitive class of rear-engined, small single-seaters.

Like the Vees, Formula Fords are a popular class with beginning drivers, but they cost more. They are also quicker, the best FF time at Lime Rock through 1969 being 92.7 mph as compared to 85.1 mph for the fastest Vee. Recently a new organization has been formed, the International Motor Sports Association, to authorize professional racing for Formula Fords.

The Formula Ford in the photograph has just won a race and is taking a victory lap. It is a Crossle, built in Ireland.

Most glamorous of all formula cars are the FIA's Formula One, or Grand Prix, racing automobiles. They compete on road circuits all over the world, one race to a country per year, to determine a World Driving Champion. Among the best known races are those at Monte Carlo, Monaco, in the spring; the Nürburgring, Germany, and Monza, Italy, in the summer; and Watkins Glen, New York, in the fall.

The current FIA formula for Grand Prix cars specifies a maximum engine size of only 183 cubic inches. This is much smaller than the 305 cubic inches of the Continental cars which Grand Prix cars resemble at first glance. Grand Prix engines are pure racing powerplants, however, hand built and of great complexity as compared to the Continental stock-block engines. Far more expensive as well, Grand Prix engines are able to produce much more power for their size. Like other formula-car engines, they run on pump gasoline.

Formula One cars are also lighter—1166 pounds minimum weight—than Formula A cars, which have a minimum weight of 1250 pounds. They are built and raced almost exclusively by factory teams such as Brabham, Lotus and March in England, Matra in France,

and Ferrari in Italy. As a result, Grand Prix cars are the most technically advanced of all racing cars, and just about the fastest on any road course.

The United States Grand Prix at Watkins Glen, New York, each October pays $50,000 for first place, more than twice as much as any other Grand Prix. Here is the winner of the 1969 USGP, Austrian Jochen Rindt, in an English Lotus-Ford. His average speed for 108 laps, nearly 250 miles, was 126.3 mph. He also turned the fastest qualifying lap at 130.1 mph.

6 / Off-Road Racing

The most recently organized form of automobile competition is off-road racing. Off-road races are not held on tracks or courses, but across the deserts of the southwestern United States or in similar areas where few people live. True to their name, off-road racers seldom use a road.

Of necessity, the cars are specially built, and very rugged. Most of them are super-tough versions of trucks, jeeps and dune buggies. There are several classes, and motorcycles also compete.

Best known of the off-road races is the Mexican 1000, or the Baja Run. Each year many entrants break down or become lost racing the length of Lower California from Ensenada to La Paz. The demanding 832-

mile route is little more than sand, ruts and sharp rocks, with an occasional washout for variety. This rough surface pounds the cars so badly that steering and suspension parts must be safety-wired so they will not loosen and drop off. Despite the terrible driving conditions, winners usually average about forty miles an hour. The photograph shows the Ford Bronco that won the 1970 Baja 500, a similar but shorter run.

Along the straight they roar, cutting and thrusting for position as they head into the turn. Out of the hole they blast, streaking down the strip in a blur of speed. Down the trail they jolt, bouncing over rocks and skidding in sand. Championship car or MG, Camaro or AA/Fueler, Grand National stocker or Baja off-roader, they are all racing cars, most dramatic of automobiles.